JUN 0 7 2012

D1575381

London's
AFTERNOON TEAS

London's
AFTERNOON TEAS

A GUIDE TO LONDON'S MOST STYLISH AND EXQUISITE TEA VENUES

SUSAN COHEN

NEW
HOLLAND

Published in 2012 by New Holland Publishers
London • Cape Town • Sydney • Auckland

www.newhollandpublishers.com

Garfield House, 86–88 Edgware Road, London W2 2EA, United Kingdom

Wembly Square, First Floor, Solan Street, Gardens, Cape Town 8000

Unit 1, 66 Gibbes Street, Chatswood, NSW 2067, Australia

218 Lake Road, Northcote, Auckland, New Zealand

ISBN 978 1 84773 993 3

Publisher: Guy Hobbs
Senior Editor: Emma Bastow
Designer: Lucy Parissi
Production: Marion Storz
Cartography: William Smuts

Printed by Toppan Leefung Printing Ltd (China)

Photography by Cath Harries, except page 35 © Dean Street Townhouse; pages 36 & 37
© The Dorchester; page 40 © Fortnum & Mason; pages 56–57 © The Lanesborough;
pages 62–63 © The May Fair; page 72–73 © The Ritz; page 80–81 © The Savoy; pages
90 & 91 © The Wolseley; pages 91–100 © New Holland Publishers.

Recipes courtesy of: page 94, Suzanne Blythin; page 97, Anne Lesker; page 98, Karen Munn;
page 101, Gunnedah Show Society.

Contents

Introduction

There is nowhere better in the world to enjoy the quintessentially English custom of afternoon tea than in London, the most vibrant and exciting capital city in the world. London has the most amazing selection of venues where you can indulge yourself and partake of anything from the most time-honoured afternoon tea to the newest twists on tradition. Tea can be a late lunch or an early supper, in which case high tea fits the bill perfectly, with savoury items to add a bit more substance.

You may be looking for a conventional afternoon tea of finger sandwiches – no crusts and there has to be cucumber – scones with lashings of clotted cream and fruity jam, followed by luscious cakes. Or you may fancy a more savoury repast. Perhaps you are searching for a tea designed with men in mind, with whisky as well as tea to drink, and heartier food, or you want one that will appeal to parents and children alike. Maybe you are after a variation on a theme, whether it be a chocaholics tea, a 'no-bread' tea, a Tea-Tox treat or a Mad Hatter's afternoon tea. Whatever your taste, London can provide it all, and in an array of interesting and exciting locations. After all, the afternoon tea experience is not just about the food you eat and the tea you drink, but also about the space and place, and here fashion and style have had a powerful influence on afternoon tea.

You can enjoy your afternoon tea in places steeped in history, from Georgian townhouses, resplendent in modern décor, to chic and buzzy bars. From elegant drawing rooms and opulent lounges in the grandest of hotels to a tiny tea shop in north London, there is somewhere to suit everyone, every pocket and every occasion. There are places with wonderful views, others with light and bright conservatories and even one, favoured by royalty, with a terrace overlooking a glorious private garden. Whether you want to linger and chat with friends, have a business meeting in relaxed surroundings, have a glorious hen do or stag event, commemorate a birthday or anniversary, collapse after a day's shopping or indulge in a pre-theatre high tea, the capital can provide the ideal venue.

Afternoon tea is the perfect way to mark those special dates in the calendar, including Valentine's Day, Mother's Day, Easter, Halloween and Christmas. Then there are annual social events, such as Wimbledon week and the Chelsea Flower Show, and many of the venues in this book offer themed teas which celebrate these particular events. This guide book is here to help you make your choice.

How afternoon tea began

The town of Tavistock in Devon has staked its claim to be the birthplace of the cream tea back in the early 11th century. The Benedictine Abbey had been looted by the Vikings in 997 AD, and a century later the monks rewarded the labourers who worked to restore it with a meal of bread, clotted cream and strawberry preserve. The Devon cream tea proved so popular that the monks continued to serve it to passing travellers long after the builders had left.

Whether Anna Maria, the seventh Duchess of Bedford, partook of scones and cream is uncertain, but according to legend, it was she who was responsible for the invention of afternoon tea as an event in the 1840s. The story goes that she was so hungry in the long gap between lunch and dinner that she ordered her maid to serve tea and cakes at five o'clock to alleviate the gnawing hunger pains. It was not long before afternoon tea became de riguer in London society. As for the drink itself, high society also played their part in making it central to the ritual. It was given the royal seal of approval by Catherine of Braganza, the Portuguese wife of King Charles II, who brought a chest of tea with her as part of her dowry in 1662. Queen Victoria's Prime Minister, William Gladstone, captured the very essence of tea when he wrote these words in 1865: 'Relaxing, refreshing, stimulating or warming, there is little to compare with the comfort and delights of a steaming pot of tea.'

There is a certain magical, even mystical quality about tea, not least of all because of the amazing influence the tiny leaf exerts on everyday life. A cup of tea is the best reason in the world to stop for a break during the day. Life's rites of passage would not be the same without tea, and the variety of leaves is such that every mood and taste can be catered for. As the world's most popular drink, tea crosses all the boundaries of history, nation, culture and class. At some time in their lives, most people acquire a taste for tea, a habit that they

rarely relinquish. The combination of a beautifully presented afternoon feast and freshly brewed leaf tea served in porcelain or bone china cups is a marriage made in heaven, and is an experience to be savoured.

The twenty-first century has seen afternoon to high standards. No longer the preserve of ladies on a shopping trip or families celebrating a special occasion, afternoon tea has become a favourite pastime enjoyed by anyone and everyone.

The synergy of design, fashion and food

'In nothing more is the English genius for domesticity more notably declared than in the institution of this festival — almost one may call it — of afternoon tea… The mere chink of cups and saucers tunes the mind to happy repose.'
GEORGE GISSING, The Private Papers of Henry Ryecroft

tea gain an unprecedented popularity, with London the mecca for this revival. Across the capital the response has been spectacular, with venues in abundance creating wonderful and often innovative menus, serving exquisite food and drink in perfect surroundings, with the expertise of professionals ensuring you enjoy the best experience possible. Many of them have won prestigious awards from the Tea Council, confirming their dedication

has had a wonderful impact and resulted in an exciting new genre, with afternoon teas on offer suited to every generation and to people from all walks of life. If you are a visitor to the capital, what better way could there be to experience this time honoured British tradition, and what better excuse could there be leave the hustle and bustle of everyday life behind for a few hours and indulge yourself?

Map of tea venues

Highgate

North Rd
Southwood Lane
16
Highgate High St
Archway Rd
Highgate Hill
Archway

Chepstow Rd
Westbourne Gr
Bishop's Bridge Rd
Queensway
Kensington Church St
Bayswater
Eastbourne Ter
Praed St
Sussex Gardens
Craven Hill Rd
Bayswater Rd
Bayswater Rd

Edgware Rd
Lisson Grove
Marylebone Rd
Gloucester Place
Baker St
Park Rd
Prince

Park Rd

Edgware Rd
Seymour St
Wigmore St
6

31   21
20

Oxford St
New Bond St
5

Park Lane
8   Mayfair

Kensington
Gardens

Hyde Park

11
12
14 17 1
22

18
Kensington Rd
Knightsbridge
Knightsbridge
Piccadilly
Green P

2 19
Belgrave
Square
Buckingham
Palace

Brompton Rd
Sloane St
Pont St

Buckingham Palace Rd
15
Eccleston

Cromwell Rd
Earl's Court

Old Brompton Rd
Fulham Rd
7
Sloane
Square
Eaton Gate
King's Rd
Warwick Wa

Warwick Rd
South Kensington
3
Sydney St
King's Rd
King's Rd
Pimlico Rd
Warwick Way

Chelsea Embankment
Grosven

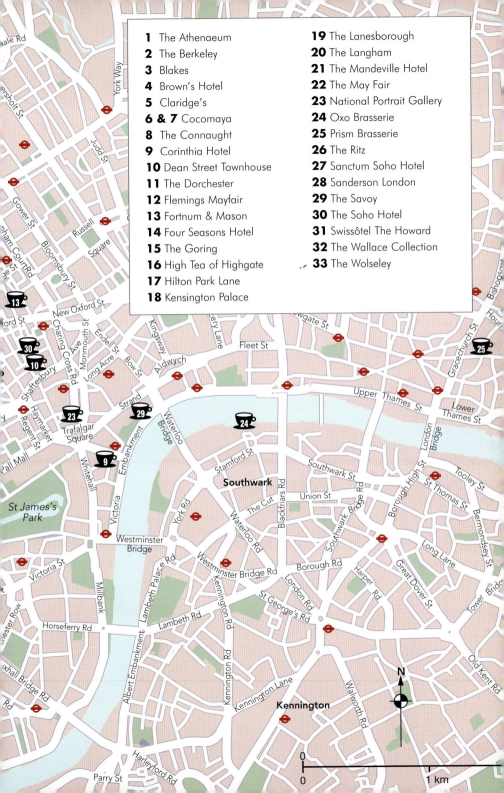

The Athenaeum

It's wonderful to step from the hustle and bustle of Piccadilly into the calm atmosphere of the luxury, family-owned Athenaeum Hotel, and to then sit back and enjoy the utterly wonderful afternoon tea on offer here. From the moment you walk into the Garden Room, with its discreet seating arrangement of rooms within a room, you can be sure of a truly memorable tea experience. Whether you are in a cosy armchair setting or with friends at one of the dining tables, the courteous staff take the greatest care of you from describing the various food courses, helping you choose which leaf tea to drink, to serving you. Everything flows at a leisurely pace and there is never the slightest hint of being rushed. Having savoured the first course of finger sandwiches, with seconds if you want, you'll have time to relax before the toasted crumpets and warm scones arrive (orange blossom are a favourite) served with the

thickest of clotted creams, lemon curd, and the fruitiest homemade jam. You'll be pleased of another break before the glass-topped cake trolley arrives with a choice of dainty pastries. The Athenaeum excels at themed teas, so do check to find out what particular treat is being featured, from a honey-lovers tea to a chocolate indulgence delight. Of course, your tea pot will be replenished with a fresh brew, and don't be afraid to try something different. The *Keemun Hoa Ya A* China special black tea, with a full bodied winey character and oaky notes, is extremely rare, and the leaves are hand sorted even before it is fired and then sorted again. Add a dash of milk and savour the wonderful flavour as you unwind.

Address: 116 Piccadilly, London W1J 7BJ

Tel: +44 (0)20 7499 3464

E-mail: dining@athenaeumhotel.com

Web: www.athenaeumhotel.com

Afternoon tea served: daily 12.30–7pm, advance booking advised

Set teas: themed afternoon teas available throughout the year

Nearest underground station: Green Park

Places of interest nearby: Buckingham Palace, Hyde Park, Green Park, Admiralty Arch

RESERVED

The Berkeley

The Caramel Room at The Berkeley, with its chocolate coloured wall coverings, snappy faux-crocodile fabrics and cool lighting is a lovely place to relax and enjoy a very special and unusual afternoon tea after a hard day out shopping or sightseeing. And what better place for a girly get-together? The set tea at The Berkeley is a fashionista's delight. Each scrumptious cake or fancy that the hotel's pastry chef produces is a miniature work of art, inspired by the themes and colours of the latest catwalk fashions. The creations, which are served on fine bone china designed by Paul Smith, have included a Philip Treacy chocolate hat cake with Monarch butterfly, an Anya Hindmarch cassis sponge tote covered in baby blue icing with iconic bow handbag, and a Christian Louboutin sparkly high-heeled ginger show biscuit with the signature red sole. Besides all these sweet delights you are offered a mouth-watering selection of little savouries, taster spoons, tea sandwiches and stylish canapés. Accompany this with a glass of Champagne, or Couture Champagne served in a Baccarat crystal glass, for the ultimate fashion accessory, and a loose leaf tea chosen from a selection which includes Ceylon, Lapsang Souchon, Pear Caramel and White Peony, and you'll want to stay all afternoon. When you do leave there is a little Prêt handbag-style take-away box in pale mint green with pink handles, which is perfect to take home any unfinished treats. And for those who live in SW1, Prêt-à-Portea can even be delivered on a fashionable customised Vespa.

Address: Wilton Place, Knightsbridge, London SW1X 7RL

Tel: + 44 (0)20 7107 8866

Web: www.the-berkeley.co.uk

Afternoon tea served: daily 1–6pm

Set teas: Prêt-à-Portea, Champagne Prêt-à-Portea, Couture Champagne Prêt-à-Portea

Nearest underground stations: Hyde Park Corner, Knightsbridge

Places of interest nearby: Harvey Nichols, Harrods, Hyde Park

Blakes

lakes, the luxury boutique hotel famously created by Anouska Hempel in 1978, is a peaceful haven in busy South Kensington, and lives up to its reputation for fine service and food. Afternoon tea is served in the stunning Chinese Room and adjoining dining room, and although they are subterranean, they are both exotic, even mysterious settings in which to enjoy a delicious and affordable repast. The added bonus here, if the weather is fine and warm, is to take tea in the delightful courtyard garden, an oasis tucked away at the back of the hotel. Expect your finger sandwiches to be served in a glass box bearing the signature B, for your mouth watering scones to be served with whipped cream, fresh strawberries and fruity jam, and to be offered a choice of cake, with a lemony Madeira and squidgy chocolate fudge being ever popular. There is a small, carefully chosen selection of teas on offer, and, unusually, Blakes pre-strain the leaves from the pot to prevent over-brewing. Dietary requirements will happily be catered for, and it is helpful to inform the hotel of these when booking.

Address: 33 Roland Gardens, London SW7 3PF

Tel: +44 (0)20 7370 6701

E-mail: blakes@blakeshotels.com

Web: www.blakeshotels.com

Afternoon tea served: daily 12.30–5.30pm

Nearest underground station: Gloucester Road

Places of interest nearby: Victoria and Albert Museum, Natural History Museum, Knightsbridge, Sloane Street, King's Road

Brown's Hotel

Afternoon tea has been served at Brown's ever since the hotel was created from four adjacent Georgian houses by Lord Byron's butler and his wife, Lady Byron's maid, in 1837. More than 170 years on, you would find it hard to surpass the quintessentially English surroundings and ambience of the Tea Room where the staff are dedicated to the highest level of service, and take care of guests with the utmost courtesy and discreet efficiency. This elegant room is a harmonious combination of contemporary furnishings, original wood panelling and open fires. The tables are set with crisp linen and fine china, and the pianist playing gently in the background creates a lovely atmosphere. The traditional tea has all the important ingredients, from finger sandwiches, super fruit and plain scones served with clotted cream and strawberry jam, to the daintiest of pastries. But there is more, for a fruity sorbet helps cleanse the palate before you try a slice of fruit cake or Victoria sponge, so-called after Queen Victoria, who often took tea here. If you are watching your waistline then Tea Tox is just the ticket, but be prepared to forego the sandwiches and scones, and instead enjoy a more savoury feast, with far fewer calories. Expect everything to be regularly replenished, for your tea pot to be refilled with the finest loose leaf tea of your choice and for your relaxing visit to last as long as

Address: 33 Albemarle Street, London W1S 4BP
Tel: +44 (0)20 7518 4155/4006
E-mail: tea.browns@roccofortecollection.com
Web: www.brownshotel.com
Afternoon tea served: Monday to Friday 3–6pm, Saturday and Sunday 1–6pm
Set teas: Traditional Afternoon Tea, Champagne Afternoon Tea, Rosé Champagne Afternoon Tea, Tea-Tox
Nearest underground stations: Piccadilly, Green Park
Places of interest nearby: Royal Academy of Arts, Green Park, St James's Park, Bond Street

you care to linger. The parting gift of a small bag of tea adds to the pleasure of the occasion. Situated in the heart of Mayfair, Brown's Hotel is a very popular haunt for visitors and locals alike, so be sure to book in advance.

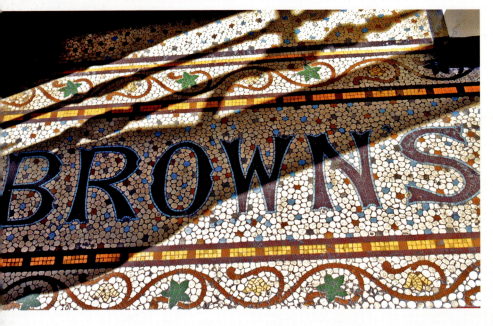

Claridge's

rt deco fans will be in seventh heaven in Claridge's, for it is a jewel of a hotel, and owes much of its splendour to the designer Basil Ionides, a 1920s pioneer of the movement. The Reading Room, with its elegant mirrors, leather banquettes, suede walls and cut marble fireplaces, is an alluring place for a very sophisticated afternoon celebration tea. Its companion room, the busier Foyer, is a dazzling space with a magnificent centrepiece. The unique silver-white light sculpture from Seattle-based artist Dale Chihuly, which hangs from the Foyer's 18 foot high ceiling, is made up of over 800 individually hand-blown and sculptured pieces and is a definite talking point.

Claridge's is justly proud of its award-winning afternoon tea. What an experience it is to have your tea presented to you on beautiful Bernardaud green and white porcelain by the impeccably-suited staff. The food is fit for royalty and is unusual without being pretentious. The set afternoon tea is designed to soothe and revive the heartiest shopper or guest; a selection of sandwiches is complemented by the most delightful raisin and apple scones, served, of course, with thick Devonshire clotted cream and its own popular tea-infused jam. Make sure you leave some room for the exquisite French pastries that follow. The selection changes daily and might include chocolate roulade, strawberry tartlets or vanilla millefeuille. The choices don't end here for besides the Champagnes on offer there are 30 different varieties of tea, selected from all over the world, to choose from. Whenever you visit Claridge's for tea there will be a pianist and violinist playing soothing music, so sit back, relax and revel in the ultimate tea experience.

Address: Brook Street, London W1A 2JQ

Tel: +44 (0)20 7107 8872

E-mail: dining@claridges.co.uk

Web: www.claridgeshoteluk.co.uk

Afternoon tea served: daily 3pm, 3.30pm, 5pm and 5.30pm

Set teas: Afternoon Tea, Champagne Afternoon Tea, Rosé Champagne Afternoon Tea, Vintage Champagne Afternoon Tea

Themed afternoon teas: Valentine's Afternoon Tea, Chelsea Flower Show Afternoon Tea, Great British Afternoon Tea

Nearest underground station: Bond Street

Places of interest nearby: Wallace Collection, Bond Street, Regent Street

Cocomaya

I t is so well worth the effort involved in finding Cocomaya, which is tucked away on Connaught Street off the Edgware Road, for it is gem of a place, and serves the most glorious afternoon tea. Cocomaya is essentially an artisanal bakery and chocolatier, open all day serving fantastic food. Every exquisite item is made in-house, including the fabulous jams. Tea can be enjoyed in either the bakery on Connaught Street, a cool neutral space with bleached wood floor and marble surfaces, or around the corner in the chocolate shop on Porchester Place, a heavenly room decorated in lime green and pink with a marvellous huge mural of a stork on one wall, and an eclectic display of vintage china. Tables are shared which makes for a very cosy, neighbourly atmosphere, but you can also book for an exclusive tea party.

Address: 12
Connaught Street
London W2 2AF

Tel: +44 (0)20 7706
2883

Address: 3 Porchester
Place, London
W2 2BS

Tel: +44 (0)20 7706
2770

Web:
www.cocomaya.co.uk

Afternoon tea served:
3pm until closing

**Nearest underground
station:** Marble Arch

'As a foreigner I find afternoon tea the most wonderful English activity. It's a meal, a celebration and a ritual all rolled into one. High tea is the jewel in the crown.'
JOEL BERNSTEIN, co-founder of Cocomaya

Wonderful food made using the finest wholesome ingredients is served on vintage china, making this a very special place. You could come here and just enjoy a cup of tea and a cake, but the set afternoon tea, which you must pre-book, is an absolute must. You get to choose the fillings for the delectable sandwiches made using artisan bread, and you'll be brought a generous selection of the bakery's beautiful cakes and yummy pastries. Don't be afraid to ask for seconds, and it is a given that what you can't eat goes home with you. There is a good selection of teas on offer and you cold round off the afternoon with a speciality

The Connaught

Tea in The Connaught's relaxed brasserie-style restaurant, Espelette, in the heart of London's Mayfair is an enlightening experience, not least of all due to the marvellous design of the conservatory. It's light and bright and you can relax and watch the world go by whilst sipping Champagne or drinking an excellent cup of leaf tea. The choice includes Royal Connaught Afternoon and Espelette Blend, as well as Silver Needle, Lapsang Imperial and Ceylon Orange Pekoe.

Luxury and style are the bywords here and are showcased in the Chic and Shock afternoon tea menu. Finger sandwiches, of course, but with fillings such as smoked

Address: Carlos Place, Mayfair, London W1K 2AL

Tel: +44 (0)20 7107 8861

E-mail: dining@the-connaught.co.uk

Web: www.the-connaught.co.uk

Afternoon tea served: Monday to Friday 3–5.30pm, Saturday and Sunday 1.30, 3.30 and 5.30pm

Set teas: Chic and Shock Afternoon Tea, Champagne (from a choice of three)

Nearest underground stations: Bond Street, Green Park

Places of interest nearby: Mayfair Village, Balenciaga and Marc Jacobs flagship stores, Bond Street, Marylebone High Street, Wallace Collection

espelette

CHIC & SHOCK AFTERNOON TEA

~oOo~

Finger Sandwiches

Olive muffin with Basque ham from Aldudes and tomato
caccia with Babaganoush, grilled Courgette and Piquillo.
e range egg with home-made mayonnaise and v
Smoked salmon and wasabi cream

salmon with a kick of wasabi cream or chicken with a 'bite' of Granny Smith apple, greek yoghurt and chives. Traditional scones are included, but the 'shock' is what the additional ones will be, perhaps melt-in-the-mouth chocolate, or fruity apricot. Whichever appears they will be served with clotted cream and a selection of the most wonderful jams by Christine Ferber. The chic pastries that follow are a picture of perfection, and for something a little less decadent, there are slices of 'proper' cake to finish with. The charming staff ensure that you have a thoroughly enjoyable afternoon.

Address: Whitehall Place, London SW1A 2BD

Tel: +44 (0)20 7321 3000

E-mail: lobbylounge@corinthia.com

Web: www.corinthia.com

Afternoon tea served: Monday to Friday 3–5.30pm, Saturday and Sunday 12–5.30pm

Nearest underground station: Embankment

Places of interest nearby: National Gallery, National Portrait Gallery, South Bank, Thames Embankment, Whitehall and 10 Downing Street, London Eye, Covent Garden

Corinthia Hotel

Through the grand entrance of this historic building, across the lobby and up the stairs into the Lobby Lounge, and you are at the very heart of the luxurious Corinthia Hotel, and in a wonderful space to indulge in afternoon tea. Understated elegance prevails, natural light floods in from the glass domed ceiling onto the fabulous Baccarat glass chandelier, and exotic flowers adorn the central table. Seated at a table set with fine linen and bespoke bone china designed by William Edwards, from your comfortable armchair you can view the peaceful courtyard, or on a warm day, where better to enjoy your tea than outside under the shade of the magnificent maple trees.

Afternoon tea here is so much more than a traditional feast. There are finger sandwiches with mouth-watering fillings, vegetarian options available, assorted scones that are crisp on the outside and light inside, and served with handmade preserves and clotted cream. Picture a perfect miniature éclair, violet iced and filled with violet cream, and you can get an idea of the exquisite pastries on your cake stand. Everything will be replenished if you so desire. Besides all this there is the Lobby Lounge Table, resplendent with hand-blown glass cake stands, each of which displays one of a selection of English tea cakes beneath the domed lid. The choice might include puff pastry Eccles cakes, which originated in Lancashire, and are filled with a mix of dried fruits, spices, apple, citrus zest and French Brandy. The apple, almond and poppy seed cake is wheat free, whilst the spicy rhubarb cake with ginger butter cream and toasted pecans is made with spelt flour, organically produced in the Cotswolds. Or you may have the chance to try the Victorian chocolate pound cake, so-called because the original 1700s recipe called for a pound each of butter, eggs, flour and sugar. Add a glass of Champagne for a special treat, and allow the trained staff to help you choose from a selection of excellent loose leaf teas from the Tea Palace — note the absence of a tea strainer — to complete the occasion. The thoughtful and attentive service includes a treat for you to take away, making this a memorable experience.

Address: 69–71 Dean Street,
London W1D 3SE

Tel: +44 (0)20 7434 1775

Web:
www.deanstreettownhouse.com

Afternoon tea served: daily
3–6pm

Set teas: Townhouse Tea and
High Tea

Nearest underground station:
Tottenham Court Road

Places of interest nearby:
Theatreland, Leicester Square,
Chinatown

Dean Street Townhouse

The Dean Street Townhouse, sympathetically converted from two four-storey Georgian properties, has a character and atmosphere all of its own that is quirky, lively and subtly stylish. Originally built in the 1730s, the houses were home to a variety of people, from aristocrats to musical publishers and Soho luminaries. Most famously the rooftop of 69 Dean Street was home to the Gargoyle club, founded in 1925, which became the in-place for London society, and was the epitome of decadent glamour. Think Fred Astaire, Francis Bacon and Lucien Freud and you get an idea of the members. Now a cool hotel, beloved of Soho socialites, film buffs and tourists alike, you can take tea in the restaurant area with its stripped wood flooring, half-panelled walls, red leather banquettes and upholstered chairs, and gaze at the contemporary art collection by Peter Blake and Tracey Emin, amongst others. Alternatively you can sit in comfy armchairs looking out onto Dean Street, or cosy-up in similar comfort in The Parlour in front of a roaring fire on a chilly day. Blue Burleigh crockery adds to the old-English feel of the place, and eager young staff will serve you a jolly good traditional afternoon tea. You may find it hard to resist adding some buttery crumpets to your order, or, if it's getting late in the day, an old-fashioned savoury delight such as macaroni cheese or yummy welsh rarebit, not to mention the fish fingers. This is very homely place to have a wonderful afternoon tea.

The Dorchester

The Promenade is at the heart of The Dorchester and afternoon tea here ranks amongst the very best that London has to offer. From the moment you cross the threshold of this stunning space, with its luxurious and elegant décor, magnificent floral arrangements and intimate seating, you can be certain of enjoying an afternoon of sheer indulgence. The ambience is relaxed, the service impeccable, and no detail has been overlooked, from the soft strains of the resident pianist, the beautiful silver-edged bone china and crisp linen tablecloths, to the silverware and fresh flowers on each table.

The Dorchester's award-winning afternoon tea, which combines tradition with innovation, is quite simply delectable. A changing selection of finger sandwiches on a variety of home-baked breads are the prelude to an amuse bouche – maybe cinnamon panacotta topped by a layer of cherry jelly. This is followed by melt-in-the-mouth scones served with both homemade strawberry and a seasonal jam, and, of course, clotted cream. The crowning glory to this mini-feast is a choice of luscious French pastries created by the pastry chef. Add a glass of Champagne to this and you have a truly celebratory tea. Whilst the most popular tea is the Dorchester House Blend, a selection of more than 20 leaf teas are available and, as you would expect from a venue of this calibre, many of these are rare varieties. If you happen to be visiting the opulent spa then you can enjoy an equally delicious variation of the Promenade menu in the calm and more intimate surroundings of the Spatisserie. It is hardly surprising that guests are as reluctant to leave The Dorchester as they are eager to arrive.

Address: Park Lane, London W1K 1QA

Tel: +44 (0)20 7629 8888

E-mail restaurant@thedorchester.com

Web: www.thedorchester.com/afternoon-tea

Afternoon tea served: The Promenade 1.15pm, 2.30pm, 3.15pm, 4.45pm and 5.15pm; The Spatisserie 3.30pm, 4.45pm and 6.45pm

Set teas: The Dorchester Afternoon Tea, Spatisserie Afternoon Tea, Spatisserie Champagne Afternoon Tea

Nearest underground station: Hyde Park Corner

Places of interest nearby: Apsley House, Buckingham Palace, Albert Memorial, Victoria and Albert Museum, Museum of Mankind, Knightsbridge, Bond Street

Flemings Mayfair

Do not be fooled by the Georgian elegance of the exterior of Fleming's, for the interior décor of the Front Room, as well as the Cocktail and Tea Rooms, is striking and sumptuous, elegant and eccentric. Both rooms are a fabulous setting for an utterly indulgent afternoon tea. Flemings pay homage to the traditional experience with their English Afternoon Tea, but with a contemporary twist. There is an excellent choice of leaf teas, tisanes and infusions, all served from an Art Deco silver tea set. From the sandwiches upwards, fluffy scones are complemented by a dainty slice of Victoria sponge, and poised temptingly on the top of the elegant cake stand is a fantastic choice of delicate pastries, including a hand-crafted cupcake from the exclusive Primrose Bakery. If you wish, you can add a glass of Champagne.

For Martini officiandos, the Fleming's signature Savoury Martini Afternoon Tea, either gin or vodka, with savoury scones, miniature scotch eggs and much more, should not be missed, but it does need to be requested in advance when you make your tea booking. So too must the Chocoholics Afternoon Tea, with it's decadent chocolate scones, a selection of chocolate cakes, petit fours, rich hot chocolate or tea. For a very special party occasion, the Pink Afternoon Tea is a girly delight, with 20 per cent of the cost being donated to the Breakthrough Breast Cancer charity.

Address: 7–12 Half Moon Street, London W1J 7BH

Tel: +44 (0)20 7499 0000

E-mail: cocktail&tearooms@flemings.co.uk

Web: www.flemings-mayfair.co.uk

Afternoon tea served: Monday to Friday 2.30–5pm, Saturday and Sunday 1.30–5pm

Set teas: Traditional English Afternoon Tea, Champagne Afternoon Tea, Chocoholic Afternoon Tea, Savoury Martini Afternoon Tea, Pink Afternoon Tea in Mayfair (for parties of 10 or more)

Nearest underground station: Green Park

Places of interest nearby: Green Park, The Royal Academy, Fortnum & Mason

Fortnum & Mason

Crossing the threshold into Fortnum & Mason, famed for its chiming clock, is like stepping into an exquisite Aladdin's cave, for the ground floor is filled with the most sublime displays of extraordinarily luxurious food. This should give you an inkling of the treat that awaits you at teatime. A number of restaurants within the store serve afternoon tea, but the most elegant is, without doubt, the spacious St James's Restaurant on the fourth floor. Here you can sit and relax in a comfortable armchair setting or, if you prefer, and specify when booking, at a more formal dining table.

The Classic and Estate afternoon teas are preceded by a choice of savoury canapés, followed a feast of finger sandwiches with an array of wonderful fillings. In traditional style, plain and fruit scones, Somerset clotted cream and a choice of Fortnum's superb preserves are next, and if you have room left, you can then choose from the appealing miniature tea cake selection. For those wanting a more substantial feast, High Tea is the obvious answer: no sandwiches here but a selection of savouries including Fortnum's famous Welsh Rarebit, muffins with poached egg or a seasonal pie. As for the tea itself, which was Fortnum's first speciality and remains close to the hearts of its customers three centuries later, the choice is exceptional and unsurpassable, and there is help on hand should you have difficulty deciding what to select. Tea guests may choose from more than seventy blends and single-estate teas sourced from all over the globe, and for the connoisseur, the chance to savour the delights of Jade Pillar, Darjeeling Autumn or other exquisite rare teas, is an opportunity not to be missed.

Address: 181 Piccadilly, London W1A 1ER

Tel: +44 (0)845 602 5694

E-mail: restaurants@fortnumandmason.co.uk

Web: www.fortnumandmason.com/afternoontea.aspx

Afternoon tea served: Monday to Saturday 12–6.30pm, Sunday 12–4.30pm, advance booking advised

Set teas: Classic Afternoon Tea, Estate Afternoon Tea, High Tea, Vegetarian, Gluten Free, Dairy Free, Diabetic, Egg Allergy, Vegan

Nearest underground stations: Green Park, Piccadilly

Places of interest nearby: Buckingham Palace, Royal Academy of Arts, Bond Street, Burlington Arcade

Four Seasons Hotel

You can enjoy your afternoon tea in any of the ground floor rooms of the beautiful Four Seasons Hotel, so choose the light and bright Amaranto Lounge with its comfortable settees and armchairs, or the richly coloured and wood-panelled restaurant if you prefer a little more formality. There are windows and mirrors galore and acres of marble, a sun-filled conservatory and even a private garden overlooking Park Lane. No need to guess how long to leave your excellent tea to brew, for you get your own special timer with enough sand to run through in two, three or four minutes, according to how strong you like it. The miniature kilner jars are novel containers for the accoutrements to your tea – clotted cream, jam and lemon curd – and the clean lines of the contemporary tiered cake stands are the perfect accompaniment for the beautiful Wedgwood china. The Italian themed La Dolce Vita is an exciting twist on afternoon tea, with savoury bites such as miniature vegetable fritto misto and mini bruschetta. There is an individual raisin and candied fruit pannettone in place of the traditional scones, and delicate regionally-influenced pastries. If you wondered what the jar of mascarpone cheese was for, then try some on the fresh strawberries sprinkled with balsamic. The Traditional Tea has lots to offer, from the sandwiches which include an egg mayonnaise and spinach roulade, the raisin and fig scones to the fruit tartlets and chocolate mousse with passion fruit. And all this while the pianist plays.

Address: Hamilton Place, Park Lane, London W1J 7DR

Tel: +44 (0)7499 0888

Web: www.fourseasons.com/london

Afternoon tea served: daily 2.30–6pm

Set teas: Traditional Afternoon tea, La Dolce Vita

Nearest underground station: Hyde Park Corner

Places of interest nearby: Apsley House, Mayfair, Hyde Park

The Goring

A mere stone's throw from Buckingham Palace and tucked away from the bustle of Victoria, The Goring is a rare treasure, for the hotel has been owned by the same family since it opened in 1910. It retains the feeling of a large, elegant private house, and every aspect of afternoon tea is intended to make it a relaxing occasion. So switch off your mobile, leave your laptop with the concierge and settle down in the cosy lounge, or in the sunny terrace overlooking the garden, and enjoy a feast fit for royalty in tranquil surroundings. Having chosen your tea from a very select list of leaf teas, including the Goring's own blend, the proceedings begin with a complementary savoury starter, made to a favourite recipe of Elizabeth, the late Queen Mother. The tiered cake stand that follows has finger sandwiches with some unusual fillings and scrumptious scones, fruit and plain, served with clotted cream and jam. The staff are always on hand to replenish your cup, refresh your pot of tea, and bring more of whatever takes your fancy. The penultimate pastry course is a treat, with dainty cakes varied according to the season, and the whole event is finished off with an individual shot glass filled with the Goring's tantalising trifle. If you happen to be visiting on a sunny summer afternoon, there is nowhere better to enjoy a truly traditional tea than seated at a table on the veranda, sipping Champagne, and enjoying the splendours of an English garden. But don't forget to ask for a table in this coveted spot when you book!

Address: 15 Beeston Place, London SW1W 0JW

Tel: +44 (0)20 7396 9000

E-mail: reception@thegoring.com

Web: www.thegoring.com

Afternoon tea served: daily 3.30–4.30pm

Set teas: Traditional Afternoon Tea, The Bollinger Tea

Nearest underground station: Victoria

Places of interest nearby: Buckingham Palace

High Tea of Highgate

Everything about this tiny tea shop on Highgate High Street is delightful, from the charming tea ladies to the scrumptious treats on offer all day long. There is a truly nostalgic air about the place and the tantalising smell of home baking as you walk in the door is enough to make your mouth water. Everything is made on the premises, and freshness and quality is the very essence of Georgina Worthington's little enterprise. Served up on chintzy china, with a cow shaped jug for the milk and satisfying amounts of thick clotted cream, the cakes and scones, sweet or savoury, flapjacks and Bara Brith (a traditional Welsh tea bread)

Address: 50 Highgate High St, Highgate Village, London N6 5HX

Tel: +44 (0)20 8348 3162

E-mail: georgina@highteaofhighgate.co.uk

Web: www.highteaofhighgate.com

Afternoon tea served: Tuesday to Thursday 11am–6pm, Friday 8.30am–6pm, Saturday and Sunday 11am–6pm (closed on Mondays)

Nearest underground station: Highgate

Places of interest nearby: Highgate Cemetery, Lauderdale House, Hampstead Heath

'Afternoon tea should be provided, fresh supplies, with thin bread-and-butter, fancy pastries, cakes, etc. being brought in as other guests arrive.' Mrs Beeton, The Book of Household Management

are scrumptious and satisfying. The regular list of cakes – including carrot, lemon drizzle, lavender sponge and chocolate orange, all displayed on cake stands under glass domes – is supplemented by daily and weekly specials, as long as they last. With an excellent selection of leaf teas to choose from, including the unusual Miss Worthington's Rose, an exquisite Rose Congou scented with rose petals, Almond Tea infused with almond pieces and essential oil, and Lavender and Rosemary, you'll be easily tempted to linger a little longer, or buy some tea to take home with you.

Hilton Park Lane

Address: 22 Park Lane, London W1K 1BE

Tel: +44 (0)20 7208 4022

E-mail: info@podium.co.uk

Web: www.podiumrestaurant.com

Afternoon tea served: daily 2–6pm

Set teas: Confessions of a Chocoholic, themed teas available throughout the year

Nearest underground station: Hyde Park Corner

Places of interest nearby: Hyde Park, Buckingham Palace, Mayfair

You don't have to be a chocolate devotee to thoroughly enjoy the excellent menu on offer at the Hilton on Park Lane, but if you are, you will certainly be in seventh heaven. Before you feast your eyes on the modern cake stand with its three courses of treats, and in a move away from the all-bread traditional finger sandwiches, you are presented with a selection of delightful open sandwiches, with vegetarian and other options available on request. You'll need plenty of room for what follows. There are scones, plain with cream and jam, as well as chocolate chip with chocolate praline spread, and then the prettiest of iced cupcakes with squidgy centres. The piece de resistance is the top tier. Perched on an edible Valrhona chocolate plate, decorated with gold leaf, are an array of picture-perfect miniature chocolate fancies which the chef changes to suit the time of year or a particular celebration, like Easter and Mothers Day, and are too good to resist. Not forgetting the fine leaf tea from Harney and Sons, chosen from a good selection, you'll have a personal timer to ensure the correct infusion time. The Podium Restaurant is a very comfortable, bustling place in which to enjoy tea for two or to have a tea party, and you can be sure of a wonderful experience.

Address: The Orangery, Kensington Palace, Kensington Gardens, London W8 4PX

Tel: +44 (0)20 3166 6112

E-mail: orangery@digbytrout.co.uk

Web: www.theorangery.uk.com

Afternoon tea served: 12–5pm or 6pm dependant on the season

Set teas: Signature Orange Tea, Enchanted Palace Tea, Royal Champagne Tea, Tregothnan English Tea

Nearest underground stations: Queensway, Gloucester Road, High Street Kensington

Places of interest nearby: Kensington Palace, Serpentine Gallery, Princess Diana Memorial Playground, Kensington Gardens

Kensington Palace

The magnificent eighteenth-century Orangery, situated within the grounds of Kensington Palace where Queen Victoria was born, is a busy and bustling place for tea, but one which still manages to retain its sense of history and grandeur. Sitting here, amidst the tranquil haven of Kensington Gardens, you can almost imagine Queen Anne and her aristocratic guests dining here in the summer months.

A heavily laden table of mouth-watering homemade scones, shortbreads, fruit slices and wholesome cakes greets you as you walk in the door and you'll find it quite a challenge deciding

what to eat. You could always go for one of the set teas rather than ordering à la carte. Besides the Signature Orange Tea, the Enchanted Palace Tea and the Royal Champagne Tea, there is the superlative Tregothnan English Tea, resplendent with tea sandwiches, mini scones with clotted cream and jam, afternoon tea cakes and dainty pastries, Champagne and, to complete the event, a choice of teas from the Cornish Tregothnan Estate. These, and a good selection of other bagged and loose leaf teas, are also on offer à la carte. The staff here are friendly and helpful, and this, as well as the close proximity of the Princess Diana Memorial Playground, helps to make the Orangery a very popular destination for families with children.

The only slight drawbacks of the Orangery are that it's so popular you may have to queue outside at busy times. This aside, you can expect to pass a very pleasant couple of hours, and you could always visit the palace afterwards.

The Lanesborough

Everything is understated luxury at The Lanesborough, from the welcome you receive on entering the hotel to the experience that awaits you taking tea in Apsleys, the beautiful glass-roofed restaurant, with its elegant décor and surroundings. The tables are set with crisp linen and bone china, gentle piano music adds to the relaxing atmosphere, and the staff are attentive and courteous. Both of

the set teas include the most appetizing finger sandwiches and bite-sized quiches, scones and miniature toasted tea cakes, as well as individual tea breads and scrummy pastries. Try some of the wonderful homemade lemon curd on your scone for a real burst of flavour. For even more of a treat have the Belgravia Tea, which starts off with strawberries and cream, and a glass of Champagne or a Kir Royal if you

Address: 1 Lanesborough Place, Hyde Park Corner, London SW1X 7TA

Tel: Apsleys +44 (0)20 7333 7254

E-mail: apsleys@lanesborough.com

Web: www.lanesborough.co.uk

Afternoon tea served: daily 4pm, 4.30pm and 5pm

Set teas: The Lanesborough Tea, The Belgravia Tea (served with Taittinger, Laurent Perrier Rose or Krug Grand Cuvee Champagne), Gluten and Dairy Free Afternoon Tea (twelve hours notice required)

Nearest underground station: Hyde Park Corner

Places of interest nearby: Hyde Park, Knightsbridge, Admiralty Arch, Apsley House

of flavour, but is there to share his expertise and guide you in your choice of leaf. The list might include Bohea Lapsang Souchong, Golden Darjeeling Okayti Estate, and a rare White Assam as well as their exclusive Afternoon Blend, consisting of Darjeeling, finest China Keemum and whole rose buds. Only leaf tea is served here, but there is not a tea strainer in sight. The secret lies in the strainer ingeniously fitted inside the silver teapot. So, whether you are exhausted from a day's shopping in nearby Knightsbridge or just want to relax, unwind or treat yourself to a glorious afternoon tea in beautiful surroundings, Apsleys is to be highly recommended.

prefer. Drinking tea here is exceptionally worthwhile, for The Lanesborough was the first London hotel to engage a Tea Sommelier, who not only tastes their teas every day to ensure quality and consistency

The Langham

The Langham has been beguiling guests since it first opened in 1865, and although the hotel is now firmly placed in the 21st century, the magnificent Palm Court pays homage to the original style and glamour. You walk through the jewelled gates into a dazzling room resplendent with silvered ceiling, art deco glass and gold encrusted walls. Beautiful Wedgwood china, crisp linen and fresh flowers adorn the tables, and the care and attention to detail makes this a wonderful experience. The most difficult thing is to decide which of the set teas to order. Each is preceded by a lovely surprise – a shot glass filled with a wonderful mousse, maybe tangy blackcurrant with a rose jelly layer on top. The scones are warm and fluffy, the sandwich selection a cut above the ordinary, and the French pastries a miniature feast. The Bijoux afternoon tea, with the most beautiful cake creations, is designed to remind you of the finest jewels, and is opulent and stylish. If you fancy High Tea, which includes mini traditional cakes – banana, carrot and fruit – and toasted crumpets as well as an additional savoury course of light, fluffy Omelette Arnold Bennett or Poached Hen's Egg Florentine, you will have to book your table for 5pm or later. As you would expect with an award-winning afternoon tea, the selection of teas on offer is exemplary, from the three Langham Blends, four Tregothnan Blends, the black, green and scented teas, as well as White, Yellow and Oolong Tea, Puerh Tea to the Tisanes. For the absolute connoisseur, the exceptional Uber Tea Selection is available at a supplement. A truly divine afternoon tea experience.

Address: 1c Portland Place, Regent Street, London W1B 1JA

Tel: +44 (0)20 7965 0195

E-mail: reservations@palm-court.co.uk

Web: www.palm-court.co.uk

Afternoon tea served: daily 2pm, 2.30pm, 4.30pm and 5pm. High tea daily 5–6.30pm

Set teas: Wonderland Afternoon Tea, The Bijoux Tea, High Tea, Tea Therapy (half day tea and spa experience)

Nearest underground station: Oxford Circus

Places of interest nearby: Oxford Street, Regent Street, Regents Park

The Mandeville Hotel

Sleek and chic, afternoon tea in the Tea Room or the deVille Restaurant at the Mandeville is a wonderfully skillful combination of the familiar and the creative. The décor here is dazzling, from the foyer with its rich furnishings, through the vibrant deVigne Bar and into the elegant and comfortable Tea Room with armchairs and settees in gloriously rich fabrics. Whether you are sitting here or in the adjacent deVille restaurant, with tables set with crisp linen and fine bone china, the tea is tremendous. The Fashion Ladies Afternoon Tea pays homage to Zandra Rhodes, from the wonderful china designed by her to the pink meringue and pink cupcakes. All the traditional elements are here – sandwiches, scones, dainty cakes and pastries – beautifully served along with a good selection of teas by Jing. Gentlemen can enjoy the especially designed afternoon tea for men, for which the Mandeville have, justifiably, earned a reputation. The Tiffany Blue china is more masculine, the sandwiches more meaty, the cakes and pastries just a bit chunkier, and the fruit cake has Buffalo Trace Bourbon in it. Besides the tea list and the Champagne, there is an excellent selection of whiskies to choose from, and if this is not enough to keep you busy, you can relax, read the paper, play a game of chess or backgammon. A final choice you could make, but only if you order it in advance, is the Chocolate Afternoon Tea. This has to be the ultimate delight for any chocoholic. Every delicate pastry, cake and scone has chocolate in it, down to the fruit skewers served with chocolate sauce. This is not for the faint hearted!

Address: Mandeville Place, London W1U 2BE

Tel: +44 (0)20 7935 5599

E-mail: sales@mandeville.co.uk

Web: www.mandeville.co.uk

Afternoon tea served: Monday to Saturday 3–5.30pm, Sunday 1–5pm

Set teas: Fashion Ladies Afternoon Tea, Men's Afternoon Tea, Chocolate Afternoon Tea

Nearest underground station: Bond Street

Places of interest nearby: The Wallace Collection, Wigmore Hall, Marylebone High Street, Bond Street, Oxford Street

The May Fair

Discretely located away from the main restaurant, Quince Salon has the feel of a private club, and is an intimate and comfortable space in which to partake of a rather different and exciting afternoon tea. Inspired by Patron Chef Silvena Rowe's Eastern Mediterranean roots, the delicate finger sandwiches are filled with savouries such as baba ganoush, avocado hummus and the mildly spiced shawarma chicken. Whilst the scones are very traditionally English, complete with clotted cream and preserves, each of the cakes and fancies has a touch of the Ottoman Empire about it. A hint of cardamom in the miniature lemon tart, a cake with fig and almond combined with white chocolate and a filo pastry made with orange and orange blossom are amongst the delicacies that will make your taste buds tingle with delight. The list of organic loose leaf tea on the menu may be small, but each is an exquisite product of the Rare Tea Company, and a treat for even the most discerning connoisseur. A glass of Duval Leroy Champagne is the perfect accompaniment to a delicious and decadent afternoon tea.

Address: Stratton Street, London W1J 8LT

Tel: +44 (0)20 7915 3892

Web: www.quincelondon.com

Afternoon tea served: Monday to Friday
3–5.30pm, Saturday and Sunday 2.30–5.30pm

Nearest underground station: Green Park

Places of interest nearby: Green Park,
Buckingham Palace, Royal Academy,
Fortnum & Mason, Bond Street

National Portrait Gallery

The vista from this restaurant, where a very good traditional afternoon tea is served every day, is not so much a portrait as a landscape, and a spectacular one at that. No matter where you sit in this stylish modern room, you get a panoramic view of Nelson's Column, Big Ben and the Houses of Parliament, which makes it one of London's wonderful hidden treasures. The Portrait Tea is a picture in itself and you get the full works – large fluffy scones, golden clotted cream and preserves, a selection of tasty house sandwiches as well as a slice of homemade cake. On the other hand, you could opt for the more glamorous Champagne Tea, with its open smoked salmon sandwich, cake, scones with all the trimmings, plus a glass of bubbly. If you are feeling very righteous, go for tea á la carte, and restrict yourself to a piece of lavender shortbread and a pot of tea. The staff are young, the service artistically indifferent and if you sit near the bar and service area, it can be a bit noisy. Still, the atmosphere is very relaxed, the tea is good and it's a super place to rest after a visit to the stunning Portrait Gallery rooms downstairs. Even on a dull wet day a visit here is an energizing experience.

Address: St Martin's Place, London WC2 0HE

Tel +44 (0)20 7312 2490

E-mail: portrait.restaurant@searcys.co.uk

Web: www.npg.org.uk

Afternoon tea served: Monday to Sunday 3.30–4.45pm

Set teas: Portrait Tea, Champagne Tea

Nearest underground stations: Leicester Square, Charing Cross

Places of interest nearby: Covent Garden, National Gallery, National Portrait Gallery, Trafalgar Square, St Martin's in the Fields

Oxo Brasserie

There is nothing ordinary about either the venue or the tea at the Oxo Brasserie, situated on the eighth floor of the Oxo Tower on the south bank of the River Thames. The breathtaking views from the amazing 250-foot terrace, combined with the contemporary décor and airy spaciousness, make this an exceptional location.

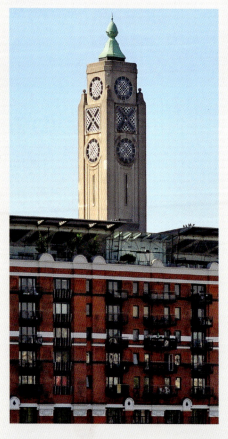

Address: Oxo Tower Wharf, South Bank London SE1 9PH

Tel: +44 (0)20 7803 3888

E-mail: oxo.reservations@harveynichols.com

Web: www.harveynichols.com/oxo-tower-london-brasserie

Afternoon tea served: daily 3.30–5.15pm

Nearest underground station: Temple

Places of interest nearby: Tate Modern, Royal Festival Hall, National Theatre, Globe Theatre

Nancy Mitford, the English aristocrat, novelist and biographer, claimed that 'milk in first', known as the MIF debate, was, without doubt, not the thing to do.

Not Afternoon Tea is just that, so don't expect scones and sandwiches but indulge yourself instead in one of the wicked pairings on offer. Combinations might be based around chocolate or rhubarb, tea and coffee, or a 'hot and sticky' theme, and each will include four picture perfect to-die-for desserts along with a carefully matched cocktail. Just thinking about a sticky toffee pudding, treacle tart, apple and pecan tartin and pear and ginger crumble is enough to set your taste buds tingling. But add to this a quirky Voodoo Child cocktail made from Havana rum shaken with cinnamon syrup, lime juice and crushed pears charged with lashings of organic ginger beer, served over crushed ice, and you'll have an idea of what is in store. Better to visit the Tate gallery before, not after, tea.

Prism Brasserie

Prism Brasserie, just a stone's throw from the magnificent Lloyds Building, and right in the heart of the City of London, is not the usual sort of place that you would expect to partake of an excellent afternoon tea. The historic building, complete with towering classical columns, was once occupied by the Bank of New York, and is now a Harvey Nichols brasserie favoured by City people. With a zinc bar, classic Mies van de Rohe 1930 'Brno' chairs in brilliant red leather and American walnut waiter stations, the large airy room is a million miles away from a traditional tea room, but this a destination worth visiting. The two set teas are served from midday

Address: 147 Leadenhall Street, London EC3V 4QT

Tel: +44 (0)20 7256 3888

Web: www.harveynichols.com/prism-london

Afternoon tea served: Monday to Friday 12–5.30 pm

Set teas: Traditional Afternoon Tea, Gentleman's Afternoon Tea

Nearest underground station: Bank

Places of interest nearby: The Bank of England, Cornhill Exchange, The Gherkin, The Lloyds Building, Leadenhall Market, The Monument. St Paul's Cathedral, Tower of London

through to 5.30pm on weekdays, are quite splendid, and very generous in proportions. If the way to a man's heart is through his stomach, then the artisan baguette filled with warm salt beef, English mustard mayonnaise and pickles accompanied by a homemade scotch egg and followed by a fruit, custard and cream dessert, should do the trick. There is no point in being on a diet if you opt for the traditional tea here for apart from fantastic sandwiches, there is proper cake, maybe Victoria sponge and carrot cake, a fresh fruit and crème patisserie tart as well as an excellent scone with clotted cream and jam and a decadent cream-filled profiterole. You'd be best to have tea after you have finished sightseeing.

The Ritz

Cesar Ritz's gracious Edwardian hotel, located in the heart of St James's, celebrated it's centenary in 2006, and is home to the world famous Palm Court. This wonderful space is the epitome of sophistication and elegance, and the afternoon tea the height of decadence and luxury. As you go up the few stairs from the ground floor central gallery area, pass between a pair of grand iconic marbled columns, and walk into the lavishly decorated and gilded Palm Court, you know that there is real treat in store. Pretty Louis XVI chairs, marble-topped tables beautifully set with crisp linen and delicate 'Ritz' bone china await the guests eager to share in what is a quintessentially Ritz experience. Whilst you relax to the delicate strains of the pianist playing, your tiered cakestand arrives with a fine selection of elegant sandwiches made using a variety of different breads – rye

for the smoked salmon and caraway seed for the cucumber – and a delectable choice of afternoon tea pastries. In pride of place on the top tier are Raspberry and Rosewater macaroons, alongside Meringue Chantilly, miniature Chocolate and Hazelnut Sponge and Vanilla Custard Slice. Warm apple and raisin scones are served with Devonshire clotted cream and organic strawberry preserve, before traditional Dundee fruit cake or classic Victoria Sponge. There are 17 splendid varieties of leaf tea to choose from, each served in an elegant silver teapot, and for that extra special celebration, your afternoon tea can be accompanied by a glass of the Ritz's own champagne.

Address: 150 Piccadilly, London W1J 9BR

Tel: +44 (0)20 7300 2345

E-mail: tea@theritzlondon.com

Web: www.theritzlondon.com

Afternoon tea served: 11.30am, 1.30pm, 3.30pm, 5.30pm, 7.30pm

Set teas: Traditional Afternoon Tea, Celebration Tea, (with or without Champagne), seasonal teas

Nearest underground stations: Green Park, Piccadilly

Places of interest nearby: Royal Academy of Arts, Green Park, Saville Row, Burlington Arcade, Bond Street

Sanctum Soho Hotel

The signature tea offering at Sanctum Soho, a boutique hotel secreted behind the façade of two Georgian townhouses, is quite different to anything else in the capital, and could stand you in good stead as late lunch or early supper. No. 20 is a terrific venue full of vintage glamour with oak floors, a dazzling bar and gold leather banquette seating providing private enclaves in which to meet friends, discuss business or just party.

> 'There is no trouble so great or grave that cannot be much diminished by a nice cup of tea.'
> BERNARD-PAUL HEROUX

Other than a steaming pot of tea, there is absolutely nothing traditional about the Gentleman's Afternoon Tea, which is a carnivore's dream from start to finish. For your first course, there are freshly prepared savouries including a rare beef sandwich, a poached oyster with bloody mary relish and a mini smoked salmon, caviar and watercress bagel. For the main course, expect the likes of a roast beef and horseradish stuffed miniature Yorkshire pudding, an individual lamb hotpot, as well as two other meaty treats. There is still dessert to follow, and if you want to move up to the fifth floor roof terrace to enjoy the twice-

Address: 20 Warwick Street, London W1B 5NF

Tel: +44 (0)20 7292 6102

Email: No.20@sanctumsoho.com

Web: www.sanctumsoho.com

Afternoon tea served: Monday to Sunday 3–5pm

Set teas: Gentleman's Afternoon Tea (a traditional afternoon tea, 'The English', is also available must be ordered when booking)

Nearest underground station: Piccadilly Circus

Places of interest nearby: Regent Street, Soho

baked chocolate fudge cake with Jack Daniels ice cream, followed by a tankard of Jack Daniels' Gentleman's Jack, you'll be in the right place to smoke the cigar which is part of the experience.

All is not lost if you happen to be accompanying a man to tea here, for the ladies can order 'The English' in advance. Love it or hate it, there are Marmite and watercress sandwiches amongst the selection served here, and if you really can't be seduced by the freshly baked scones, clotted cream and Tiptree Little Scarlet jam, then there is another touch of nostalgia to tempt you – hot buttered crumpets.

Sanctum Soho successfully blends tradition with cutting edge style, and the menus, especially the Gentleman's Tea, are strikingly innovative.

Sanderson London

Fortunately there is no need to go down a rabbit hole to enjoy this fairytale experience, just a requirement that you join in the fun. Alice in Wonderland would be thrilled by this quirky afternoon tea, and have been tempted to say 'curiouser and curiouser' as she finished off the contents of the bottle marked 'Drink me'. A wonderful concoction of flavours – such as apple pie, lemon curd and English toffee – linger in the mouth as you try to identify each one. The rainbow-coloured finger sandwiches – cucumber and black pepper on beetroot bread is one – are a feast for the eyes and the tummy, and the scones are, well, fluffy and light as air. Fancy cakes are designed to remind you of characters like the White Rabbit with an individual chocolate cake which looks like a pocket watch, and the Queen of Hearts, which begs you, in icing,

to 'Eat Me.' A hazelnut praline ice cream lollipop explodes with a single bite, and a twirl of a fruit flavoured one will turn your mouth from hot to cold. On warm days you can take tea in the landscaped inner courtyard, on others sit in the bustling, modern Suka restaurant, with its mix of tables and chairs or long tables and high stools. An unusual tea which delights children and adults alike, and one which is great fun for a celebration and will make you grin like the Cheshire cat.

Address: 50 Berners Street, London W1T 3NG

Tel: +44 (0)20 7300 1400

Web: www.sandersonlondon.com

Afternoon tea served: Monday to Friday 2.30–5.30pm, Saturday and Sunday 1–5.30pm

Set teas: Mad Hatter's Tea

Nearest underground station: Tottenham Court Road, Goodge Street

Places of interest nearby: Soho, Oxford Street

The Savoy

As you descend the elegant staircase to the Thames Foyer of the Savoy you can't help but notice an aura of restrained elegance and grandeur. Light floods in from the great glass cupola above you, and music played by the resident pianist drifts across the room. The tranquil ambience is complemented by the discreet but attentive service and guests may linger in the deep sofas and armchairs, or at their table, for as long as they like. The set tea of delicate finger sandwiches, plain and fruit scones served with clotted cream and strawberry preserve, bite-size French pastries, and a choice of The Savoy's signature cakes is a delight. Don't worry if you can't finish everything – a doggy bag can easily be arranged! For those with a bigger appetite the Savoy High Tea is wonderful, for it combines elements of the traditional afternoon tea with more substantial food. Follow your sandwiches with toasted crumpets instead of scones, and enjoy smoked salmon and scrambled

Address: Strand, London WC2R 0EU

Tel: +44 (0)20 7420 2111

E-mail: savoy.dining@fairmont.com

Web: www.fairmont.com/savoy

Afternoon tea served: daily 2.30–6.30pm

Set teas: Traditional Afternoon Tea,
Traditional High Tea

Nearest underground stations: Covent Garden,
Embankment

Places of interest nearby: Somerset House,
Royal Festival Hall, National Theatre, Savoy
Theatre, Covent Garden, Royal Opera House

eggs served with melba toast before you indulge in a slice of cake – carrot with cream cheese icing, lemon and poppy seed or rich English fruit. Connoisseurs of tea will be spoilt for choice as the Savoy offers a distinctive collection of leaf teas. Besides their own special blend – a robust black tea blended from Indian, Kenyan and Sri Lankan leaves – there are three Savoy Favourites; Tiger Hill (a Nilgiri Hills tea), Lapsang Souchon Butterfly and Fairmont Earl Grey. Add to these a choice of green teas, green flavoured teas, Oolong, Darjeeling – Margaret's Hope and Castelton, a premium second flush tea – Assam and Ceylon teas, as well as black flavoured teas, decaffeinated teas, white tea and a selection of herbal and fruit infusions, you realize that tea is taken very seriously here. And before you leave, do pay a visit to the in-house shop, Savoy Tea, where you can purchase any of the teas in specially designed caddies, a copy of Anton Edelman's book, *Taking Tea at the Savoy*, or even another pastry to take home. Pure extravagance.

The Soho Hotel

Situated in a quiet mews off Dean Street, the Soho Hotel is as surprising as it is sophisticated, spacious and incredibly stylish. The décor is a quirky mix of traditional English furniture and vibrant modern fabrics, with an eclectic display of artworks adorning the walls. If you like to be in a space humming with activity, then ask for a table in the Refuel bar and restaurant. For a more peaceful, relaxing ambience book your table in the elegant drawing room with its hugely inviting sofas, or in the comfort of the wood panelled library. Each of the afternoon teas is wonderful, from the Traditional with its delicious finger sandwiches, super scones with the essential clotted cream and jam, and delectable cakes, to the Champagne Tea, with the addition of smoked salmon blinis and a bowl of strawberries. Even the cake stands make a statement here, for they are modern, bordered in pink or green to match the décor. But the star turn has to be the Ruinart and Miller Harris Sensory Tea, which combines food with more delicate

flavours such as cucumber and basil sandwiches, a dainty raspberry tartlet and a lemon cupcake, all designed to complement the freshness of the Blanc de Blancs Champagne and the Miller Harris fragrant teas. Sipping Thé Petales, a delicate pure blend of Vanilla Ceylon and Rose Absolute from Turkey, from a Wedgwood Wild Strawberry bone china tea cup is a real joy. For a fabulous treat, why not book seats for the Sunday afternoon Film Club, watch the movie of the week in one of the state-of-the-art screening rooms, and then enjoy a blissful Champagne Tea. This is somewhere where you could really spend all day.

Address: 4 Richmond Mews, London W1D 3DH

Tel: +44 (0)20 7559 3000

E-mail: refuel@sohohotel.com

Web: www.firmdale.com

Set teas: Traditional Tea, Champagne Tea, Fruit Tea, Ruinart and Miller Harris Sensory, Seasonal teas, Film Club with afternoon tea.

Nearest underground station: Tottenham Court Road

Places of interest nearby: Oxford Street, Bloomsbury, British Museum, Soho, China Town

The Wallace Collection

What more stunning venue could there be for tea in Central London than The Wallace, the restaurant situated in the beautiful Sculpture Garden of Hertford House, home to the Wallace Art Collection? As you make your way to the informal but elegant restaurant, you can't help but notice the wonderful paintings by artists such as Titian, Rembrandt, Hals (The Laughing Cavalier) and Velázquez. Seated at tables amongst beautiful trees beneath the fabulous glass atrium roof, this is a positively charming place to while away an hour or so. Choose your set tea from the classic Cornish to the not-so-traditional English with it's devilled Cromer crab on melba toast. Or you could go continental and indulge in the Parisian tea and feast on homemade foie gras, salmon tartare and goose rillette followed by French fancies and pastries. Add your choice of tea from the list of more than 20 loose leaf on offer – including favourites like Darjeeling and Assam and the more unusual China White Silver needles – and maybe a glass of Champagne, and you are all set for a last look at the exquisite art collection on your way out.

Address: Hertford House, Manchester Square, London W1U 3BN

Tel: +44 (0)20 7563 9505

E-mail: reservations@thewallacerestaurant.com

Web: www.wallacecollection.org

Afternoon tea served: daily 3–4.30pm

Set teas: Cornish Cream Tea, English Afternoon Tea, The Parisian

Nearest underground stations: Bond Street, Baker Street

Plces of interest nearby: Wallace Collection, Bond Street, Oxford Street

Address: 160 Piccadilly, London W1J 9EB

Tel: +44 (0)20 7499 6996

Web: www.thewolseley.com

Afternoon tea served: Monday to Friday 3–6 pm, Saturday 3.30–5.30pm, Sunday 3.30–6.30pm

Set teas: Cream tea, Afternoon Tea, Champagne Afternoon Tea

Nearest underground station: Green Park

Places of interest nearby: Green Park, The Royal Academy, Fortnum & Mason, Bond Street

The Wolseley

Ever since The Wolseley opened its doors in November 1993, it has gained a reputation as one of the most stylish restaurants in London. It is hard to believe that this magnificent Grade II listed building, with the grand pillars, marble floors, sweeping staircases and loggias was originally designed in the 1920s as a prestigious car showroom, but such is the evolution of the building. Now a Grand Café, the place positively hums with activity all day long, so don't expect to sit in peace and quiet here. The staff are very attentive, and will happily bring you a newspaper whilst you wait for your friend to arrive!

Afternooon tea is served in the tea room and the main restaurant and the set afternoon tea, on its tiered stand, is as traditional as it comes. There is a selection of finger sandwiches, excellent fruit scones and a selection of pastries and cakes, or you can opt for just scones and cream, or decide to have just cake and tea. The small selection of leaf teas includes the The Wolseley's own Afternoon Blend, English Breakfast, Earl Grey, Darjeeling, Ceylon, Assam, Jasmine and Green. A favourite with celebrities, you never know who'll you'll be sitting next to.

Victoria Sponge

Serves 8

175 g (6 oz) butter, plus extra for greasing
175 g (6 oz) caster sugar
3 eggs, beaten
175 g (6 oz) self-raising flour, sifted
1 teaspoon baking powder

Filling
300 g (10 oz) good-quality strawberry jam
300 ml (10 fl oz) double cream, whipped to
**   soft peaks**
icing sugar, for dusting

Preheat the oven to 180°C/350°F/gas 4. Grease two 20-cm (8-inch) sandwich tins and line with greaseproof paper.

Using an electric whisk, beat together the butter and sugar until the mixture looks pale and fluffy. Gradually add in the beaten eggs, beating well between each addition, then fold in the flour. Divide the mixture evenly between the two tins and place in the oven for about 20 minutes, or until firm to the touch and golden in colour. Leave to cool in the tins for a minute and then carefully turn out onto a wire rack to cool completely.

Spread the flat side of one of the cold sponges with the jam. Spread the flat side of the other with the whipped cream. Place the sponges carefully together and press down gently. Dust the top with extra icing sugar.

Scones

Makes 10–12 scones

225 g (8 oz) self-raising flour, plus extra for
    dusting
pinch of salt
55 g (2 oz) cold butter, cut into cubes
25 g (1 oz) caster sugar
150 ml (5 fl oz) milk

To serve
clotted cream
jam

Preheat the oven to 220°C/425°F/gas 7. Lightly dust a baking tray with flour.

Sift the flour and salt into a bowl. Using your fingertips, lightly rub the butter into the flour until the mixture resembles breadcrumbs. Add the sugar and the milk and lightly mix until just combined.

Tip the mixture out onto a lightly floured work surface. Using the palm of your hand, flatten out the dough out until it is about 2 cm (1 inch) thick. Cut out 10–12 scones using a 5-cm (2-inch) cutter.

Place the scones on to the baking tray and bake for 12–15 minutes, or until the scones are golden-brown and well-risen. Remove from the oven and place onto a wire rack to cool.

Serve the scones with clotted cream and your favourite jam.

Salmon & Cucumber Sandwiches

Makes 12 dainty sandwiches

1 tablespoon good-quality mayonnaise

2 teaspoons baby capers, chopped

1 teaspoon chopped fresh dill

4 slices soft white fresh bread, lightly
   buttered

50-100 g (1½–3½ oz) smoked salmon or
   smoked trout

¼ small or English cucumber, finely sliced

freshly ground black pepper

Combine the mayonnaise, chopped capers and dill together in a small bowl and spread over two of the slices of white bread.

Place generous amounts of the smoked salmon or trout on top.

Overlap nine thin slices of cucumber until it is covering the salmon and then season with freshly ground black pepper.

Top with second slice of fresh bread and then carefully trim the crusts off each sandwich. Cut each one into three fingers, then cut each finger in half.

Date, Fruit & Nut Loaf

Serves 6–8

175 g (6 oz) dates, nuts and/or sultanas,
 or a mixture of all three.
200 ml (7 fl oz) boiling water,
125 g (4 oz) butter or margarine
1 teaspoon bicarbonate soda
200 g (7 oz) plain flour
150 g (5 oz) sugar
1 teaspoon baking powder
1 egg

Preheat the oven to 180°C/350°F/gas 4 and lightly grease a loaf tin.

In a large bowl, mix together the dates and nuts, water, butter or margarine and bicarbonate soda and leave to cool for a few minutes.

Add the plain flour, sugar, baking powder and bind together with the egg. Stir until well combined.

Pour the mixture into your prepared tin and cook in the oven for 40–45 minutes.

Perfect Pavlova

Makes 10–12 small pavlovas

6 egg whites
225 g (8 oz) caster sugar
1 teaspoon cornflour
1 teaspoon white vinegar
½ teaspoon vanilla essence
300ml (10fl oz) thickened cream
2 tablespoons icing sugar
seasonal fruit, to decorate

Preheat the oven to 120°C/250°F/gas 1. Grease a large baking sheet and line with greaseproof paper.

Using an electric beater, beat egg whites in a clean, dry bowl until soft peaks form.

Gradually add the sugar, beating well between each addition, until the meringue is thick and glossy, and all sugar is dissolved. Add the cornflour, vinegar and vanilla essence and fold through the mixture with a spatula.

Place spoonfuls of the meringue mixture onto the baking sheet using a tablespoon. Don't worry too much about creating perfect shapes – just try and get them evenly round. Bake in the oven for 1½ hours or until the meringue is dry to the touch. (Do not open oven during cooking.)

Turn off the oven, leaving pavlova inside with the door ajar until completely cool. When cool, carefully remove from the baking paper and transfer to serving plate. Alternatively these can be stored in airtight container until required.

Using an electric beater, beat the cream and icing sugar until peaks form. Spoon cream carefully onto pavlova and decorate with any fruit you like.

Melting Moments

Makes about 20

185 g (6 oz) butter
60 g (2 oz) icing sugar
60 g (2 oz) custard powder
185 g (6 oz) plain flour
½ teaspoon vanilla extract

Lemon filling
75 g (2½ oz) butter
90 g (3 oz) icing sugar
zest of 1 lemon
2 teaspoons lemon juice

Preheat oven to 180°C/350°F/gas 4.

Cream together the butter and sugar. Add custard powder, flour and vanilla extract; mix well.

Roll the firm paste into small balls and press down with a fork onto a baking tray lined with grease proof paper. Bake for approximately 8 minutes until pale golden brown.

To make the lemon filling, beat all ingredients together to combine.

When biscuits are cooked and cooled, spread one biscuit with a tablespoon of filling and top with another biscuit.

ADDRESSES, WEBSITES & TRANSPORT LINKS

The Athenaeum, page 12
116 Piccadilly, W1J 7BJ
www.athenaeumhotel.com
TUBE: Green Park

The Berkeley, page 16
Wilton Place, Knightsbridge SW1X 7RL
www.the-berkeley.co.uk
TUBE: Hyde Park Corner, Knightsbridge

Blakes, page 18
33 Roland Gardens, SW7 3PF
www.blakeshotels.com
TUBE: Gloucester Road

Brown's Hotel, page 20
33 Albemarle Street, W1S 4BP
www.brownshotel.com
TUBE: Piccadilly, Green Park

Claridge's, page 23
Brook Street, W1A 2JQ
www.claridgeshoteluk.co.uk
TUBE: Bond Street

Cocomaya, page 26
12 Connaught Street, W2 2AF
186 Pavilion Road, SW1X 0BJ
www.cocomaya.co.uk
TUBE: Marble Arch

The Connaught, page 29
Carlos Place, W1K 2AL
www.the-connaught.co.uk
TUBE: Bond Street, Green Park

Corinthia Hotel, page 32
Whitehall Place, SW1A 2BD
www.corinthia.com
TUBE: Embankment

Dean Street Townhouse, page 34
69–71 Dean Street, W1D 3SE
www.deanstreettownhouse.com
TUBE: Tottenham Court Road

The Dorchester, page 36
Park Lane, W1K 1QA
www.thedorchester.com
TUBE: Hyde Park Corner

Flemings Mayfair, page 38
8–12 Half Moon Street, W1J 7BH
www.flemings-mayfair.co.uk
TUBE: Green Park

Fortnum & Mason, page 40
181 Piccadilly, W1A 1ER
www.fortnumandmason.com
TUBE: Green Park, Piccadilly